Bitch Slap MLA

NATHANIEL SIMMONS, PH.D.

JOHN C. BYERLY

ISBN: 1976345820
ISBN-13: 978-1976345821

Printed by Kindle Direct Publishing, An Amazon.com Company.
Available on Kindle, Amazon.com, and other retail outlets.

Facebook: @bslapMLA
Instagram: @BitchSlapMLA

DEDICATION

To those who have been bitch slapped by MLA format,
may you now BITCH SLAP MLA!

CONTENTS

Acknowledgments   i

1   WTF is MLA   1

2   Fucking Fundamentals & Mechanical Bull Shit   3

3   The First Damn Page   12

4   Making a Bad Ass Works Cited   14

5   In-text Citations & Shit   21

6   Mother Fucking MLA Examples   24

7   Annotated List of Works Cited Shit   46

8   10 Common Fuck Ups   49

9   Sample Paper   51

ACKNOWLEDGMENTS

Special thanks to those who supported Bitch Slap APA. Your support encouraged this fucking book! Thanks bitches, now Bitch Slap MLA!

1

WTF IS MLA

The Modern Language Association (MLA) created a way to format our shit and get all of our ducks in a row when writing papers, essays, and research. They call this "MLA format." Your professors and employers will refer to this as "MLA." So, MLA made MLA for MLA to confuse us all. The liberal arts and humanities (and a few other fuckers) use MLA as their standard for formatting papers.

So, why do I need this shit, you ask? If you're a student, because your teacher, professor, college, or university fucking said so. If that's the case, buck up and do your shit so that you can get the fuck outta Dodge! Everything has hoops. Life is one big fucking hoop. Your job will have hoops. Jump pony jump. But, don't just jump, show them that you can do fucking backflips.

If you're just another nerd like Dr. Simmons… well you need this shit to publish your research in certain journals (even though they might do an abridged MLA). Further, if you like things to look pretty and enjoy being told what to the fuck to do, then MLA is for you! As one of our English professors would always say, "We need a common way to look up research." In other words, if you follow MLA correctly, we will all understand how to locate the book, magazine, journal article, etc. and won't be wondering what the hell you are talking about and if we can even find whatever it is the fuck you were trying to write. It makes that shit nice and tidy! However, this doesn't mean MLA is nice, or easy.

MLA is a bitch. So, you better bitch slap it before it bitch slaps you! Follow our instructions. We know our shit and will tell you what the fuck to do and how the hell to do it. So listen up! And fucking try! No one likes a bitch who doesn't try.

So, how the hell do I use this book? This book isn't necessarily meant to be read cover to cover. Instead, look up what shit you need and save yourself some fucking time.

Chapter Two covers the fucking fundamentals and mechanical bull shit of MLA. In chapter two, you will learn about basic shit such as levels of heading, what fucking font to use, and how the hell your paper should look in MLA format. This chapter also tells you the basic shit you need to know about punctuation, block quotes, parentheses, and capitalization, etc. It's annoying as hell, but it's the way MLA is, so follow our fucking advice.

Chapter Three reviews the first damn page. Essentially, in chapter three, you will learn how the hell your first damn page should look. It is really that fucking simple.

Chapter Four tells you how to make the baddest bad ass works cited ever. We share what the fuck to include within your works cited list and tips to guide your works cited list construction. There's even an example as to what this shit should look like.

Chapter Five covers in-text citations and related shit. Learn how to cite in-text one or multiple fucking authors.

Chapter Six perhaps lists more mother fucking MLA examples than you might want. We offer works cited examples for all sorts of shit like books, journals, and online newspaper articles.

Chapter Seven reveals how to annotate your works cited based off MLA sensibilities. For whatever reason, MLA doesn't share how the hell to make an annotated works cited in their handbook, so we guide you on what an annotation might look like.

Chapter Eight reviews 10 common fuck ups that are common within MLA users. Here, you will learn ways to NOT fuck it up, as you work towards being a bitch slapping goddess. BAM!

Chapter Nine shares snapshots from a bull shit sample paper. Within those snapshots, you'll see visual examples of items discussed in this book such as levels of heading and a works cited page.

2

FUCKING FUNDAMENTALS &
MECHANICAL BULL SHIT

Welcome to MLA Fucking Fundamentals 101. In this chapter, we discuss what the fuck to do about your font, spacing, margins, and so forth. Wanna know how to list levels of heading in MLA? Then, this chapter is for you bitch. Lost already? No worries, cozy on up to MLA like it is your next casual encounter and let's get this shit done.

The eighth edition of MLA tries to make shit simplistic by giving us three fucking guidelines to live by:

1. We should cite simple shit shared by most works such as an author and title.
2. We should remember that there is more than one damn way to document a source.
3. We should make our citing fucking useful to others.

Font
The MLA font of choice is Times New Roman, 12 point font. We wrote this fucking book in Times New Roman to help you know what it looks like. Sometimes people might be down with Calibri because that is

usually the default now in Microsoft Word. After all, MLA says to use something legible, but whatever – stick with Times New Roman and don't be a whiny little dick.

Spacing
Double-space your shit! Yes, all of it! Enough said.

Spacing after punctuation
Space only one damn time after periods, question marks, and other types of fucking punctuation marks. Obviously, your boss or professor may have other things in mind. When in doubt, ask them. Otherwise, go with this MLA shit. We double spaced our shit in this book because it is fucking easier to read. You're welcome.

Margins
Margins should be one-inch all around. One fucking inch!

Indentation
Always fucking indent the first line of paragraphs one half-inch. MLA says to use the damn tab key and not the space bar to indent. Do people seriously use the fucking space bar to indent? Bitch please! Use the damn tab!

Italics
Italics can help your fucking readers fucking understand. MLA tells us that there are specific ways we should use this shit.

Use italics for:

- Titles such as *Bitch Slap MLA* or our other book *Bitch Slap APA.*
- To make your shit *fucking* sparkle for emphasis.
- To italicize any foreign words your reader won't fucking know. You know, when you're trying to look smart as hell by using multiple languages. Like you do…well, don't do this for common foreign words such as amigo, gimme a fucking siesta, and laissez-faire. You know, shit like that.

Title Page
WTF? MLA says no! Don't have a fucking title page. If you really want a title page go do APA or some other shit like that…

Author Info
Since there is no damn title page, you should write your name, your instructor's name, the course, and the date in the upper left-hand corner of the first mother-fucking page. This shit needs to be double-spaced.

John C. Byerly

Dr. Nathaniel Simmons

BITCH SLAP 101

19 September 2019

Headings
You can number or not number your section headings, just follow this simple bad ass example on pugs (because pugs fuckin' rock!).

1. Pugs
2. Colors of Pugs
2.1 Fawn Pugs
2.2 Apricot Pugs
3. Pug Personalities

Do you want the sleek as fuck unnumbered look? Well, there are five possible formatting ways to organize your headings within your paper.

Following this fucking format for your levels of heading:

1. **Flush that shit left. Make it bold.**
2. *Italicize that shit and flush it to the left.*
3. **Center that shit. Make it bold.**
4. *Italicize that shit and center it too.*
5. <u>Underline that shit and flush it to the left.</u>

Note: We added the (1, 2, etc.) to demonstrate the level of heading for clarity. **Don't put the (1, 2, etc.) after your title dumbass, just do what it says.** That's not fucking MLA, that's us helping you to fucking bitch slap the hell out of it!

Pugs (1)

Colors of Pugs (2)

Fawn Pugs (3)

Personalities of Fawn Pugs (4)

Fawn Pugs are the Shit (5)

Apricot Pugs (3)

Page Numbers
In your upper-right damn header, put your last name, followed by a fucking space, and then number all of your shit consecutively. You know, like 1, 2, 3, shit like that. This needs to be on-half of a fucking inch from the top and flush to the mother-fucking right.

Endnotes
If you use this shit, put it on a separate page before the damn Works Cited page. This damn page should be titled "Notes" and centered. Only one damn note in your list? Then call it "Note." Remember to:

- Number your shit (e.g. 1, 2, 3...).

  Example:
  Some fucking scholars argued fuckers fuck.[1]

- That numbers should fucking match up. So, if you labeled an endnote with a 1 in text, then in your Notes it should also be labeled 1. This shit is common sense. Connect the dots mother fuckers.

  Example:
  Some fucking scholars argued fuckers fuck.[1]
  1. See Simmons, especially chapter 5, for more on this shit.

- Double space the damn notes.
- Indent the first line of each endnote with five fucking spaces. Subsequent fuckers should be flush to the left.
- Don't forget your fucking period and space after each damn endnote.

MLA doesn't like long bull shit notes. However, they do like short bibliographic notes which refer people to other fucking work or explanatory notes which is where you fucking explain your shit.

Bibliographic note example:

1. See Simmons, especially chapter 5, for more on this shit.

2. For a contrasting view on the importance of bitch slapping, see Smith 50; Doe 2-10.

3. Other studies back up my shit. See Byerly and Simmons 30-50, Doe, 55-76.

Explanatory note example:

4. In 2000, this fucker interviewed with some famous person and said, "I am a bad ass!" (Smith 150).

Numbers
Follow this fucking advice for when you gotta count shit.

- Use fucking lowercase roman numerals for book pages that use this shit. For example: page xxx
- People that were unfortunate enough to not have a unique name should also have roman numerals to clarify who the fuck you're talking about. For example: Sammy IV
- If you have a big ass number, it is fucking ok to use numbers and words together. For example, I won the fucking lottery and now have 545 million bucks! (Don't I fucking wish?!).
- For page numbers, MLA doesn't want you to list shit such as "page, p., or pp." Go use APA or some other shit like that, if you wanna travel that lonely road.

Quotation Marks ""
Wanna make shit sparkle or stand the fuck out? Then, you may use quotation marks for that shit to signal your bad ass misuse or your special meaning. Also, you might see some academic bull shitters claim to "coin" a "new" term. They'll sometimes put quotes around that shit to make it snappy.

NATHANIEL SIMMONS, PH.D. & JOHN C. BYERLY

Square Brackets []

Use this shit instead of two sets of parenthesis. Like fucking so: This is fucking boring, so why should I (give a [flying] fuck) care.

Short quotes

Short quotes are usually three to four fucking typed lines or less. As a general fucking rule, think of short quotations as four or less lines of text (AKA mother fucking prose) and three or less lines of fucking verse. Just put your shit in quotation marks and in-text cite it like you would normally. And don't forget your fucking punctuation after your citation! No citation? Then, put your punctuation within your quotation makes. "It is this fucking simple."

If you're citing some shitty ass poetry, mark the breaks within the quotations with a slash (/). If you have a fucking stanza, use a double slash (//). If you don't know what the fuck this means, then you don't fucking need it. Count your blessings.

Simmons said, "Of all the bull shit here / There's more there" (5-6).

Long quotes

If you're citing lots of shit, then you're gonna need to follow the rules for a long ass quote. Some people might refer to this as a fucking block quote. As a general fucking rule, think of long quotations as more than four lines of text (AKA "prose" by stuck up fuckers) or more than three lines of verse.

Shit to remember:

- Long ass quotes should start on a new line and all that shit should be indented a half inch from the left margin.
- Keep double-spacing, as that is the fucking rule.
- Cite your shit after the punctuation mark of the quote.
- If you quote verse, keep the original fucking line breaks.

*Notice that this long shit doesn't need quotation marks around it.

Simmons found the following:

ALTs might also benefit by increasing their knowledge of their host

country's conceptions of privacy in preparation for immigration.

Providing intercultural training on both sides of this interpersonal, intercultural relationship will provide participants with tools and vital information as they navigate such interactions. (33)

*Notice that the period in a block quote is also at the end of the sentence instead of after the parentheses. Don't fuck this up!

Want to add shit to quotations?
Just put your words in fucking [brackets]. Doing so indicates that it is not part of the original fucking text. Using the same quote from above, let's see how many times we can add [fucking].

Simmons found the following:

ALTs might also [fucking] benefit by increasing their [fucking] knowledge of their host country's conceptions of privacy in preparation for immigration [and shit like that]. Providing [fucking] intercultural training on both sides of this [fucking] interpersonal, intercultural relationship will provide participants with [fucking] tools and [fucking] vital information as they navigate such interactions. (33)

Want to take shit out of your quotations? Then just use an ellipsis . . . Simmons found the following:

ALTs might also benefit by increasing their knowledge of their host country's conceptions of privacy in preparation for immigration. Providing intercultural training. . . will provide participants with tools and vital information as they navigate such interactions. (33)

<u>Fucking Reminder</u>: If you use an ellipsis at the end of a fucking sentence, then you gotta put punctuation still. So, yes, this might mean that you have four damn periods in a row. It makes sense though. Would you fucking eat the last piece of pizza? Yes! Then, don't leave this mother fucker out in the cold either. Don't forget your damn punctuation.

Abbreviations

MLA uses fucking abbreviations all the damn time in works cited and in-text citations. You shouldn't fucking use them anywhere else. It's important to keep this shit crystal clear so people know WTH you are talking about.

- Don't use periods or spaces between abbreviations that are almost all capital fucking letters
    o DVD, PhD, US, and shit like that.
- Abbreviated names don't have spaces, unless it is a full damn name
    o JFK and N. P. P. Simmons are both correct.
- Lower-cased abbreviations end in a damn period.
    o pp. vol. ed. and shit like that.
- However, if your lowercase abbreviations mean more than one word, then you need a period between that shit.
    o p.m., i.e., e.g., and shit like that.

Common Fucking Abbreviations

The MLA Handbook has a complete list of all the damn abbreviations, but here are a fucking few to get you started.

- anon.   anonymous
- ch.   chapter
- dept.   department
- ed.   edition
- e.g.   for example
- et al.   and others
- etc.   and so forth
- i.e.   that is
- jour.   journal
- lib.   library
- no.   number
- P   Press
- p., pp.   page, pages

- par.   paragraph
- qtd. in   quoted in
- rev.   revised
- sec.   section
- ser.   series
- trans.   translation
- U   University
- UP   University Press
- var.   variant
- vol.   volume

In your damn works cited...

- Months that are longer than four fucking letters should be abbreviated.
  - Jan., Feb., Mar., and shit like that.
- Country, province, and state names should be fucking abbreviated.
  - Columbus, OH; London, Eng.
- Write the entire name of publishers who are not fucking popular. In other words, don't make shit up, cuz we won't know who the fuck you're talking about.
- Leave out shit like Corp., Inc., Co., and Ltd. – no one gives a damn.
- Use U and P when talking about fucking university presses (e.g. Bitch Slap UP or U of Bitch Slap P).

3

THE FIRST DAMN PAGE

MLA doesn't have fucking title pages. Sure, your boss or professor might ask you for one. In that case, just do whatever the hell they want to make them happy. Just know deep in your heart that they are fucking wrong. In short, you will need author information, a fancy ass title, and a header with page number. This chapter tells you what the fuck to do on your first damn page and even shows you a mother-fucking example of how the hell it should look.

Author Information
Since there is no damn title page, you should write your name, your instructor's name, the course, and the date in the upper left-hand corner. This shit needs to be double-spaced, like so:

John C. Byerly

Dr. Nathaniel Simmons

BITCH SLAP 101

19 September 2019

Fancy Ass Title
Then, you're going to need a bad ass, mother-fucking title – centered below that.

Header with Page Numbers (AKA Running Head)
In your upper-right damn header, put your last name, followed by a fucking space, and then number all of your shit consecutively. You know, like 1, 2, 3, shit like that. This needs to be one half of a fucking inch from the top and flush to the mother-fucking right. There's just one damn space between your last name and the page number.

Here's an example of all this bull shit:

Byerly 1

John C. Byerly

Dr. Nathaniel Simmons

BITCH SLAP 101

19 September 2019

Fancy Ass Title

Bull shit. Bull shit.

Bull shit. Bull shit.

Bull shit. Bull shit.

Bull shit. Bull shit. Bull shit. Bull shit. Bull shit. Bull shit. Bull shit. Bull shit. Bull shit. Bull shit. Bull shit. Bull shit. Bull shit. Bull shit. Bull shit. Bull shit. Bull shit. Bull shit. Bull shit.

4

MAKING A BAD ASS WORKS CITED

MLA calls a bibliography or reference list "works cited." Don't fuck this up. It's important to use the language of the style guide. Is it the same shit? Absofuckinglutely, but fucking this up can make you look like a dip shit.

General Shit
- This should be in ABC fucking order!
- No author? Don't ever use *Anonymous* or *Anon.*, dammit!
- No one fucking cares about anyone's Ph.D., JD, MD, whatever the fuck they throw after their name to look fancy. Leave it the fuck out.
- MLA does give a fuck about people who have been cursed with names that end in Jr., Sr., III, IVIVIVI, or shit like that. Don't do that to your fucking kids. It ain't right.

Works Cited Components
Generally, each entry in your works cited should have an author, publication year, title, and publisher information. Publisher information might be the name of a formal publishing company like in a book, but it might also be a type of sponsoring organization like a newspaper name.

Specifically, MLA requires that we have core fucking elements such as:

1. Author
2. Title of source
3. Title of container
4. Other contributors
5. Version
6. Number
7. Publisher
8. Publication date
9. Location

As an author, it is your responsibility to make sure things are fucking right. Don't make us search because you fucked it up and left some shit out!

Author

All this shit goes in ABC order and it is alphabetized by the author's last name. Authors' names should be written last name first and then the first name. Put a fuckin' comma after the last name and a period after the first name, like so:

Simmons, Nathaniel.

If any author takes the damn time to tell you their middle name, list it – even if it is just a middle initial.

Byerly, John C.

Got two fuckin' authors? That's cool. Sometimes people do that shit. Take the fucking authors of this book for example (i.e., Nathaniel Simmons and John C. Byerly). We become:

Simmons, Nathaniel, and John C. Byerly.

*Notice that only the first author is last name first. The second author is written as one might expect, if they were writing their own damn name on a piece of paper. It's that fucking simple.

Got three fuckin' authors? MLA makes our life somewhat easy with this shit. Rather than list them all out, we get to peace the fuck out after writing *et al.*

Simons, Nathaniel, et al.
Byerly, John C., et al.

Got the same damn author?
Then, order that shit by the title and use three fucking hyphens for the author's name for every entry after the first damn one.

Simmons, Nathaniel. A Bull Shit Story.

---. A Cunning Tale of Bull Shit.

Editors
Sometimes books have editors. Editors are bastards that get all of the money for the book, while individual chapter authors get a line on their resume that they wrote some shit. Editors do also add a fucking coherent voice and oversee the quality of the pieces, but yes...they get the fucking money in the end. Chapter authors don't get shit. MLA likes to call out these greedy bastards by labeling them as "editor" after their name.

Byerly, John C., editor.
Simmons, Nathaniel, editor.

Title of source
After the fucking author/editor's name, add the damn title. You will use italics or quotation marks depending upon the shitty source type.

For books, make it italics:

Simmons, Nathaniel. *Gaijin Private Parts: Maintaining Privacy at*

Work in Japan.

For websites, put that shit in italics:

Simmons, Nathaniel. "How to Bitch Slap MLA." *Bitch Slap MLA*,

www.bitchslapmla.com/how_to_bs_mla.html.

Periodicals (you know, magazines, journals, newspapers, shit like that...), **gets quotation marks:**

Simmons, Nathaniel. "Bull Shit Titles: Keeping it Real." *Bull Shit*

Studies, vol. 12, no. 1, 2019, pp. 5-10.

Songs/Music get quotation marks too:

Sally. "Get it Girl." Work, Fake Entertainment, 2018,

www.sallythesingerisnotreal.com/album/work-get-it/.

Title of container

WTF are "containers?" Well, it's something you put your shit into. For MLA, containers are essentially the same damn thing. Containers are the larger shit that contains the information you want. For example, if you want to fucking cite an episode of your favorite series, the individual episode is the source and the series is your fucking container. The title of containers are usually fucking italicized. Make sure to also capitalize each fucking word, unless it is an article, preposition, or conjunction.

Simmons, Nathaniel. "Bull Shit." *The Bitch Slap Bull Shit Series of*

Contemporary Short Stories, edited by John C. Byerly, Sage, 2000,

pp. 34-54.

Other contributors

Sometimes authors need a little fucking help. Thus, they get some damn contributors. These bitches might be called "editors, illustrators, translators, etc."

Simmons, Nathaniel. *Madness and Other Fuckery: A History of*

Nonsense. Translated by John C. Byerly, Random House, 2005.

Version

If a source lists an edition or version, then fucking include it. It's that damn simple.

Simmons, Nathaniel, and John C. Byerly. *The Bull Shit Bible*. Fucking

Hell Version, Oxford UP, 2018.

Simmons, Nathaniel, and John C. Byerly. *The Bull Shit Bible*. 3rd ed.,

Oxford UP, 2018.

Number
Sometimes there is additional shit you need to add such as a volume or issue number. Seasons in TV shows are also fucking numbered (i.e., season 5, episode 2).

Simmons, Nathaniel. "Bull Shit Titles: Keeping it Real." *Bull Shit*

Studies, vol. 12, no. 1, 2019, pp. 5-10.

Publisher
Publishers produce and distribute shit. This is essentially your friendly neighborhood drug dealer.

Simmons, Nathaniel and John C. Byerly, *Bitch Slap Comedy*. Bitch Slap

Studios, 2017.

MLA also lets you abbreviate shit. So, for example, if you are using a book from Random House Publishers, you can just write Random House. It saves you some time for video games and shit.

Remember this shit: You don't need a fucking publisher's name with sources such as periodicals, shit published by their author or editor, websites that are named the same damn thing as their publisher, websites that make their shit available but don't publish them (such as WordPress, YouTube, and shit like that).

Publication date
This is the date your shitty source is published. Sometimes there are multiple fucking dates. In this case, just use the date that is most relevant to you (special thanks for your fucking vagueness MLA!). If you're confused as fuck, then use the shitty source's original publication date.

Simmons, Nathaniel and John C. Byerly, *Bitch Slap Comedy*. Bitch Slap

Studios, 2017.

No fucking date? Then, MLA let's you speculate some shit. If you do, speculate, put some shitty ass brackets around it.

[*circa* 1969] means it is a fucking estimated date.
[1969?] means that you don't have a fucking clue, but you're trying.

Location
The location is where you can find the shit. This might be page numbers, the URL (don't forget to remove the fucking http:// or https:// shit), or physical location like the Museum of Modern Art, New York.

URLs
MLA says that you should put in the same fucking URL you see in your browser, unless your fucking source has a DOI or a permalink.

How should this shit look?
The works cited page should be at the end of your paper, after any fucking endnotes. It should have the same running head as the rest of the damn paper. Write the words "Works Cited" on the top of your page. Don't forget to center that shit.

Here's a fucking example to help you visualize this shit:

Simmons 11

Works Cited

Byerly, John C. "American Bull Shit." Review of *Basic Bitches*, by Nathaniel Simmons. *New Beginnings*, vol. 10, Mar. 2007, pp. 55-57.

Simmons, Nathaniel. Introduction. *Bad Ass Writing*, by John C. Byerly, 2nd ed., U of Fuck You P, 2005, pp. i-iii.

WTF is a DOI?
A DOI stands for "digital object identifier." It is essentially a way to find electronically-stored shit. Think of it as the fucking social security number for journal articles. Add DOIs, if you fucking have them. You can put a damn doi instead of a fucking URL, if you want. Use this fucking format for DOI numbers in your works cited:

doi:xxx
*Notice that there is no fucking space between the colon and number.

Don't fucking flip out if the DOI is hellishly long. They do that shit to piss you off.

Date of Access

The date of access, access dates, or accessed dates refer to when the hell you looked at this shit. These are not fucking required, but they are encouraged when there's no damn copyright date. You can also use this as a fucking optional piece of shit, if you think it'll help others. Access dates can be handy as hell for online shit, because we all remember that one video that went MIA as fuck that one time we tried showing it to our friend. Shit comes and goes online, so it can be helpful to note when the fuck you looked at it.

Here's a fucking example:

So, if you looked at a website on Halloween in 2019, you should write:

Accessed 31 Oct. 2019.

Just tack that shit on the end of your reference in your works cited page, like so:

Byerly, John C. "Title of Some Shit: My Shit Don't Smell." *Healthy Shit*,

20 Jan. 2020, madeup.com/getitgirl.htm. Accessed 5 May 2021.

5

IN-TEXT CITATIONS & SHIT

In-text citations are a fucking brief reference in your writing that shows where the fuck you got your shit. In-text citations are also called parenthetical citations. You should have in-text citations for things you directly quote and even for ideas you paraphrased.

Basic Shit
Basic shit is that your in-text citation needs the author's name and the page number in parentheses, like so:

Bull shit is "the shit we make up" (Simmons 4).

Or, you can also write shit like this:

According to John C. Byerly, bull shit is "fucking shit we make up" (5).

Two Authors
Got two damn authors? This is simple shit. Just add both names with the word "and" between them. We added onto the example above to give a mother-fucking example of this:

Bull shit is "the shit we make up" (Byerly and Simmons 4).

Or, you can also write shit like this:

According to Byerly and Simmons, bull shit is "fucking shit we make up" (5).

Three or more Authors
Some authors like to cluster together and write lots of shit. In that case, you list just the first author's last name and then use et al. For example:

Simmons et al.
Bull shit is "the shit we make up" (Byerly et al. 4).

Or, you can also write shit like this:

According to Byerly et al., bull shit is "fucking shit we make up" (5).

Corporate Authors
Sometimes authors are corporations or large organizations such as the National Society of Bull Shit. Just put that shit where you would the author name like in the "Basic Shit" example above. MLA encourages abbreviating long titles to not mess with people's grove as they are reading. In other words, it can be a fucking distraction to keep reading "National Society of Bull Shit." So, you could write Nat'l Society of Bull Shit.

No Fucking Author
This shit drives me crazy too, but MLA tells us what the fuck to do. If someone forgot to write their name on their paper… they seriously didn't learn that shit in pre-school?! --- well, if someone forgot to write their name on their paper, AKA there is NO FUCKING AUTHOR, then use a short ass version of the work's title. Add a page number, if it fucking exists.

Some old white ass mother fucker mansplained "Blah Blah Blah…" ("The Impact of White Mansplaining" 5).

This means "The Impact of White Mansplaining" is the title. 5 is the page number.

Multiple Works by the Same Author
Authors are busy fuckers. So, they sometimes have multiple shit published. Here are two damn good ways to do this. First, shorten the

title and use the shortened titles in quotation marks (unless the title is already fucking short!), like so:

Simmons and Byerly argued blah blah blah ("Bitch Slap APA" 38). Further, Simmons and Byerly claimed blah blah blah ("Bitch Slap MLA" 3).

Secondly, if you don't want to write the fucking author's name in a sentence, then you can put it into the citation, along with the title, and page number.

Blah blah blah (Simmons and Byerly, "Bitch Slap MLA" 3).

Indirect (Or Secondary) Sources
You should always try your fucking best to cite original work. However, sometimes that shit just isn't possible. In that case use "qtd. in" to show where the fuck you always got your shit.

Byerly described "blah bull shit blah" (qtd. in Simmons 235).

Works with Multiple Editions
You always need a damn page number, but sometimes you run into shit that has all sorts of volumes, etc. So, if you're citing some fancy literary work with a shit ton of editions. Here is WTF you do:

- List the damn page number.
- Add a semicolon.
- Then, abbreviate whatever the fuck you are citing such as a book (bk.), chapter (ch.), section (sec.), volume (vol.), or paragraph (par.).

Blah blah blah, some fancy pants shit here (83; vol. 3).

Multiple Citations
Sometimes it helps to make your point fly as fuck when you say what multiple people say. In other words, these peeps are backing up your shit multiple times. You list them in ABC order inside your bad ass parentheses. Just separate that shit with a semicolon, like so:

(Byerly 55; Simmons 5).

6

MOTHER FUCKING MLA EXAMPLES

This chapter will contain the best mother fucking examples you've ever seen. Bluntly, your life will be fucking changed as you learn how to make a kick ass MLA works cited that's almost as perfect as pugs! Read carefully and pay god damn good attention. Don't mess this shit up. It's so easy, even a broke ass bitch could do it.

Follow the fucking format below. Look for the relevant information and plug it in. This shit is that easy.

You might be asking, can't I just use an online system to cite? Fuck no! They NEVER EVER, NEVER EVER WORK!! Do they work?! NO, they fucking don't!! Don't even think about trying that shit! It's a gateway drug to fucking up!

*Disclaimer: Not all the examples are legit research articles, books, and shit like that. We made some of this shit up because we got tired of spending too damn long looking for fucking legit items that were interesting. Deal w/ it. See, we are so tired after all this we can't even write "with!"

Index for Mother Fucking MLA Examples

Books, Book Chapters, & Reference Books
1. Book, no author
2. Book, one author
3. Book, one author with only one name
4. Book with two authors
5. Book with three or more authors
6. Same author, multiple works
7. Book with an editor
8. Book of poems or short stories
9. Book with a corporate author or organization
10. Books with editions
11. Translated book
12. Book volume(s)
13. Introduction, Preface, Foreword, or Afterword
14. Reviews
15. Religious books
16. Reference books

Periodicals
17. Journal article
18. Journal article from an online database
19. Article with two authors
20. Article with three or more authors
21. Journal article, online-only
22. Journal article, forthcoming
23. Special issue journal article
24. Magazine article
25. Magazine article, online
26. Newspaper article
27. Newspaper article, online
28. Editorial
29. Pamphlet
30. Government publication

Unpublished & Informally Published Manuscripts or Works
31. Interviews
32. Personal Communication
33. Lectures, Speeches, or Oral Presentations
34. PowerPoint Slide

Electronic Sources
    35. Websites
    36. Page within a website
    37. E-mail
    38. Online comment
    39. Online discussion group
    40. Electronic mailing lists
    41. Blog post
    42. Twitter/Tweets
    43. YouTube videos

Meetings & Symposium
    44. Conference presentations
    45. Conference proceedings

Doctoral Dissertations & Master's Theses
    46. Master's thesis, unpublished
    47. Master's thesis, published
    48. Doctoral dissertation, unpublished
    49. Doctoral dissertation, published

Audiovisual Media & Art
    50. Netflix and chill, Hulu, or Google Play
    51. Television episode
    52. Television series
    53. Specific performance or part of a TV show
    54. Broadcast TV or radio program
    55. Music Videos
    56. Sound Recordings
    57. Films, videos, or movies
    58. Performances
    59. Podcast
    60. Song or album
    61. Painting, sculpture, or photograph

Books, Book Chapters, & Reference Books

Fucking Format:
The author's last and first names are written out fully. Don't abbreviate that shit! Italicize the fucking title. Add the publisher and the damn date it was published AKA the mother fucking publication date.

Last Name, First Name. *Title of Work.* Publisher, Publication Date.

1. **Book, no author**

   Stories of Fucking Awesome Pugs. Hoover UP, 2019.

2. **Book, one author**

   Visage, Michelle. *The Diva Rules: Ditch the Drama, Find your Strength, and Sparkle your Way to the Top.* Chronicle, 2015.

3. **Book, one author with only one name**

   RuPaul. *Workin' it!: RuPaul's Guide to Life, Liberty, and the Pursuit of Style.* It Books, 2010.

4. **Book with two authors**

   Simmons, Nathaniel, and John C. Byerly. *Keeping it Real.* Fake Shit, 2016.

5. **Book with three or more authors**

   Beck, Christina, et al. *Celebrity Health Narratives and the Public Health.* McFarland, 2015.

6. **Same author, multiple works**
   List this shit by ABC order. Save yourself from fucking carpal tunnel and use three hyphens and a period for the second and beyond entry. This is a book example, but this hyphen shit works for all multi-work shit by the same damn person.

   Simmons, Nathaniel, and John C. Byerly. *Keeping it Real.* Fake

   Shit, 2016.

   ---. *Keeping it Real Too.* Fake Shit, 2017.

7. **Book with an Editor**
   Dependent upon how you used the work, will depend on how you cite this shit.

   Citing an edited work?

   Byerly, John, editor. *Forty Years of Bitch Slapping Advice.* Sage,

   2021.

   Citing just one bit inside an edited work? Then, do it like this bitch:

   Simmons, Nathaniel. "Bitch Slapping School." *Surviving Life,*

   edited by John C. Byerly, Fake Press, 2020, pp. 10-21.

8. **Book of Poems or Short Stories**

   Simmons, Nathaniel. "To Bull Shit or Not Bull Shit." *Life*

   Relevant Poetry, Fake UP, 2020, pp. 25.

   *Got an editor? Just add that shit.

   Simmons, Nathaniel. "Pugs not Drugs." *Vintage Pug Poetry,*

   edited by John C. Byerly, Fake Press, 2020, pp. 5-7.

9. **Book with a Corporate Author or Organization**

Bull Shit Association. *Teaching Children Bull Shit*. Random

   Pool, 2020.

*WTF do I do if my organization and publisher are the same damn thing? This bitch. Skip the damn author, list the damn title first and then list the author as the publisher.

Bull Shitting Ohio Style. Columbus Bull Shit Association, 2020.

10. **Books with Editions**

Condon, John, and Tomoko Masumoto. *With Respect to the*

   Japanese: Going to Work in Japan. 2nd ed. Intercultural

   P, 2011.

11. **Translated Book**

Simmons, Nathaniel. *Bitch Slaps & Shit*. Translated by John C.

   Byerly, Fake Books, 2015.

12. **Book Volume(s)**

Just one fucking volume:

Byerly, John, C. *Bull Shit Tips and Tricks*. Edited by Nathaniel

   Simmons, vol. 69, Random UP, 2000.

More than one fucking volume:

Byerly, John, C. *Bull Shit for Children*. Edited by Nathaniel

   Simmons, Random UP, 2000. 4 vols.

13. Introduction, Preface, Foreword, or Afterword

Simmons, Nathaniel. Introduction. *Bad Ass Writing*, by John C.

Byerly, 2nd ed., U of Fuck You P, 2005, pp. i-iii.

14. Reviews (books, plays, films, shit like that)

Fucking Format:
Reviewer's Last Name, Reviewer's First Name, "Title of

Review." Review of *Title of the Work*, by Author,

Publication Title, Publication Date, Pages.

Byerly, John C. "American Bull Shit." Review of *Basic Bitches*,

directed by Nathaniel Simmons. *Columbus Times*, 5 Mar.

2007, p. A5.

Simmons, Nathaniel. Review of *Bitch Slap MLA*, edited by

Grace Smith and John Sake. *Life Supplement*, 20 Mar. 2019,

p. 57.

15. Religious Books

The Bible. New International Version, Oxford UP, 2001.

16. Reference Books (e.g. encyclopedias, dictionaries, similar shit).

For these, leave out the damn publisher. No one gives a fuck.

When ya got a damn author:

Smith, Kelly. "Anus." *Encyclopedia of Anatomy*. 10th ed., 2000.

When there is no fucking author:

"Bull Shit." *Encyclopedia of Life*, 2nd ed., 2000.

Periodicals

Periodicals are basically the shit that is published regularly (i.e., newspapers, newsletters, magazines, and journals).

Fucking Tip:
- If there is no issue number, don't freak the fuck out. Just don't list one. It's that fucking simple.
- Accessed dates are not fucking required, but they are encouraged when there's no damn copyright date.
- Add dois if you fucking have them.

Fucking Format:
Author. "Title." *Journal Name*, vol. XX, no. X, Year, pp. XXX-XXX.

   doi:XXXXXX

17. Journal Article

Simmons, Nathaniel. "Speaking like a Queen in RuPaul's Drag

   Race: Towards a Speech Code of American Drag

   Queens." *Sexuality & Culture,* vol. 18, no. 3, 2014, pp.

   630-648. doi:10.1007/s12119-013-9213-2

*Is this shit online too? This works too:

Simmons, Nathaniel. "Speaking like a Queen in RuPaul's Drag

   Race: Towards a Speech Code of American Drag

   Queens." *Sexuality & Culture,* vol. 18, no. 3, 2014, pp.

   630-648, www.thisisit.edu/article/3433. Accessed 3 June

   2015.

*Just remove the page numbers above, if this bitch isn't in print too.

18. Journal Article from an Online Database
WTF is an online database? LexisNexis, JSTOR, shit like that.

Simmons, Nathaniel. "Speaking like a Queen in RuPaul's Drag

Race: Towards a Speech Code of American Drag

Queens." *Sexuality & Culture,* vol. 18, no. 3, 7 Dec.

2013, pp. 630-648. *JSTOR,* doi:10.1007/s12119-013-

9213-2.

*Only add the access date if you fucking want to. We didn't.

19. Article with two authors

Simmons, Nathaniel, and Yea-Wen Chen. "Using Six-Word

Memoirs to Increase Cultural Identity Awareness."

Communication Teacher, vol. 28, 2014, pp. 20-25.

doi:10.1080/17404622.2013.839050

20. Article with three or more authors

Beck, Christina S., et al. "Blurring Personal Health and Public

Priorities: An Analysis of Celebrity Health Narratives in

the Public Sphere." *Health Communication,* vol. 29, no.

3, 2014, pp. 244-256. doi:10.1080/2012.741668

21. **Journal Article, online-only** (not in print)

Simmons, Nathaniel. "The Tales of *Gaijin*: Health Privacy

Perspectives of Foreign English Teachers in Japan."

Kaleidoscope, vol. 11, 2012.

opensiuc.lib.siu.edu/cgi/viewcontent.cgi?article=1087&c

ontext=kaleidoscope. Accessed 20 Nov. 2013.

22. **Journal article, forthcoming**

Simmons, Nathaniel. (forthcoming). "Cultural Discourses of

Privacy: Interrogating Globalized Workplace

Relationships in Japan." *Journal of International &*

Intercultural Communication.

23. **Special issue journal article**

Simmons, Nathaniel. "Fake Title Bitches." *Bull Shit and Society*,

special issue of Journal of Bull Shit, vol. 4, no. 2, 1969,

pp. 100-110.

*Web entries should include a fucking URL, DOI, or permalink.
Just tack that shit on the end.

24. **Magazine article**

Byerly, John C. "Title of Some Shit: My Shit Don't Smell."

Healthy Shit, 22 Feb. 2005, pp. 28-30.

25. Magazine article, online

Byerly, John C. "Title of Some Shit: My Shit Don't Smell."

Healthy Shit, 20 Jan. 2020, madeup.com/getitgirl.htm.

Accessed 5 May 2021.

26. Newspaper article

Simmons, Nathaniel. "Using Swear Words to Convey Meaning."

Fuck it Times, 22 Feb. 2015, p. A1, A5.

27. Newspaper article, online

Currie-Robson, Craig. "Teachers Tread Water in *Eikaiwa*

Limbo." *The Japan Times.* 22 Jan. 2014,

www.japantimes.co.jp/community/2014/01/22/general/te

achers-tread-water-in-eikaiwa-limbo/#.UxyVV4XskY2.

Accessed 5 June 2017.

28. Editorial

Suzuki, Harumi. "The Art of Bull Shit." Editorial. *Newsweek*, 1

Feb. 2000, p. 20.

"The Art of Bull Shit." Editorial. *Newsweek*, 1 Feb. 2000, p. 22.

29. Pamphlet

Bitch Slapping Rights. Ohio Department of Social Services,

2010.

30. Government Publication

United States, Congress, Senate, Committee on Fuckery.

Hearing on the Chaos. Government Printing Office,

2010. 112th Congress, 2nd session, Senate Report 444-3.

United States, Department of Bull Shit. *Managing Bull Shit: A*

Guide to MLA. Government Printing Office, 2010.

Unpublished & Informally Published Manuscripts or Works

Unpublished manuscripts are manuscripts that people were too lazy to publish. JK. This is shit that might be in progress, meaning it is in the fucking works, so chill! It might have been submitted to a journal, and some of those journals are as slow as molasses on a fucking cold night! This could also be work on a personal website – basically, nowhere real fucking formal, just a chill place to share yo' business.

31. Interviews
These fuckers might be in print, broadcast, or unpublished.

Personal Interview Example:
Simmons, Nathaniel. Personal interview. 12 Sept. 2017.

Published Interview Example:
Byerly, John C. Interview with Nathaniel Simmons. *Ohio*

Review, vol. 12, no. 2, 2017, pp. 15-20.

Simmons, Nathaniel. "Fuck You." *Interviews with USA's Bad*

Asses, By John C. Byerly, Fake P, 2000.

Online-only Published Interview Example:

Byerly, John C. Interview by Nathaniel Simmons. *Using Cuss Words Effectively*, 20, Apr. 2001, www.fake.com/en/unow.blah. Accessed 10 May 2019.

32. Personal Communication

See #31 for Interviews.

See #37 for Emails.

33. Lectures, Speeches, or Oral Presentations

Simmons, Nathaniel. "Intercultural Privacy Management." National Communication Association Annual Conference, 10 Nov. 2000, Hilton Hotel, Chicago, IL. Keynote Address.

Simmons, Nathaniel. "Sexual Health Disclosure." Communication Studies 101. Ohio University, 10 Nov. 2000, Lasher Hall, Athens, OH. Lecture.

34. PowerPoint Slides

Simmons, Nathaniel. MLA 101: Bitch Slap MLA, 3 Apr. 2011, Bitch Slap University, Seattle.

For a single slide:

Simmons, Nathaniel. "MLA Bitch Slap Goals." MLA 101: Bitch Slap MLA, 3 Apr. 2011, Bitch Slap University, Seattle. Slide 3.

Electronic Sources

Fucking Format:
Electronic sources are crazy as fuck. MLA still follows the basic shit of "Author, Title of source, Title of Container, Other contributors, Version, Number, Publisher, Publication Date, Location" and shit like that. Because each damn source can look different, see the fuck below for examples of how the hell to do it.

Fucking Tips:
- No page numbers? Then use par. or pars. which stands for the fucking paragraph number. Don't ever fucking use p. or pp.
- No author? Use the user name, if one exists.
- When listing a URL, don't put the damn https://, MLA knows that fucking exists. Save yourself some carpal tunnel.
- If there's a fucking permalink or a shortened version of the URL, use that shit.
- Accessed dates are not fucking required, but they are encouraged when there's no damn copyright date.
- Add dois if you fucking have them. You can put a damn doi instead of a fucking URL, if you want.

35. Websites (as in the entire damn site)
Access dates are fucking optional in MLA, but some people want this shit, so we included it below so you can see what it fucking looks like.

Bitch Slap MLA. The MLA Manual with a Bad Fucking Mouth,

2018, bslapmla.edu/werkbitch. Accessed 22 Jan. 2017.

Simmons, Nathaniel. *Guide to Bitch Slapping MLA.* Bitch Slap

U, 20 Jan. 2018, www.badassu.edu/mla/. Accessed 5 May

2005.

36. **Page within a Website** (some specific shit)

If the author is fucking known:

Byerly, John C. "Making Tang Cookies." *Delicious Bitch*,

www.deliciousbitch.com/tang/cookies. Accessed 20 Feb.

2011.

For MIA as fuck authors:

"History." *JET Programme*. 20 Nov. 2011,

www.jetprogramme.org/e/introduction/history.htm.

37. **E-mail**

Byerly, John C. "Re: Bitch Slap APA." Received by Nathaniel

Simmons, 25 Sept. 2018.

38. **Online Comment**

SmartASS69. Comment on "Shut the Hell Up!" CNN, 10 Aug.

2017, 6:00 p.m., cnn.com/US/storytime23432.

39. **Online Discussion Group**

SmartFucker [John C. Byerly]. "Re: Citing MLA format

efficiently." *MLA Assistance*, 2 Dec. 2000.

groups.mla.com/fake/url/loveit.html. Accessed 2 Feb.

2010.

40. Electronic Mailing List (AKA a listserv)

Simmons, Nathaniel. "Re: Bitch Slapping MLA." *MLA Help*, 20

        Feb. 2011, lists.bitchsla/making/this/up.htm. Accessed

        22 Feb. 2012.

41. Blog Post

Simmons, Nathaniel. "Health Privacy in Japan." 14 Aug. 2015,

        jetwit.com/wordpress/2015/08/14/jets-in-academia-

        health-privacy-in-japan/. Accessed 5 Mar. 2017.

42. Twitter/Tweets

@bitchslapmla. "This MLA shit ain't rocket science." *Twitter*,

        20 Feb. 2015, 5:00 p.m., twitter.com/bitchslapmla/no/343.

43. YouTube Videos

When uploaded by some other bitch:

Bitch Slap APA. "Happy as Fuck." *YouTube,* uploaded by

        Nathaniel Simmons, 5 Mar. 2002,

        www.youtube.com/aasdfasdfasdf.

When the author's name and the uploader are the same fucking
person:

"Happy as Hell." *YouTube,* uploaded by Bitch Slap APA, 10

        Mar. 2002, www.youtube.com/aasdfas555.

Meetings & Symposium
Academics have to present their shit to other academics in order to increase their reputation and keep their fucking jobs. Here is how the fuck you cite this shit when you wanna look fly as fuck.

44. Conference Presentations

Cite like Lectures, Speeches, or Oral Presentations #33.

45. Conference Proceedings

Simmons, Nathaniel, et al., editors. *Proceedings of the Tenth*

Annual Meeting of Bitch Slappers Society, March 3-6,

2005: General Session on Bitch Slapping. Bitch Slappers

Society, 2007.

Wanna cite only a section of this shit? Then, do this the same damn way you would an essay in a collection.

Byerly, John C. "Bitch Slapping Patterns in Academic Writing."

Proceedings of the Tenth Annual Meeting of Bitch Slappers

Society, March 3-6, 2005: General Session on Bitch

Slapping, edited by Nathaniel Simmons et al., Bitch

Slappers Society, 2007, pp.500-10.

Doctoral Dissertations & Master's Theses

Fucking Format:
Dissertations and theses are a lot of work and so you can find this shit in all sorts of places (i.e., personal websites, databases, etc.). However, MLA says wherever the hell you find it, you should cite it like a book.

46. Master's thesis, unpublished

Simmons, Nathaniel. "Unrequited Love: A Communication

Perspective." MA thesis, Missouri State University, 2007.

47. Master's thesis, published

Simmons, Nathaniel. *Unrequited Love: A Communication

Perspective.* MA thesis, Missouri State University, 2007.

UMI, 2009.

48. Doctoral dissertation, unpublished

Simmons, Nathaniel. "Negotiating Boundaries in a Globalized

World: Communication Privacy Management between

Foreign English Teachers and Japanese Co-Workers in

Japan." Dissertation, Ohio University, 2014.

49. Doctoral dissertation, published

Simmons, Nathaniel. *Negotiating Boundaries in a Globalized

World: Communication Privacy Management between

Foreign English Teachers and Japanese Co-Workers in

Japan.* Dissertation, Ohio University, 2014. UMI, 2016.

AAT 5861458

Audiovisual Media & Art

Fucking Format:
From Netflix and chill to your favorite TV shows, songs, and art, this shit
can all look fucking different, but remember to keep in mind MLA's

guidelines for "Author, Title of source, Title of Container, Other contributors, Version, Number, Publisher, Publication Date, Location" and shit like that.

50. Netflix and chill, Hulu, Google Play (shit like that)

"Zero Fucks." *Not Giving a Shit*, season 3, episode 10, ABC, 20

Mar. 2018. *Netflix*, www.netflix.com/watch/234534/fake.

51. Television Episode

"Who farted?" *Life with Fuckers: The Complete Fifth Season*,

created by Nathaniel Simmons, performance by John C.

Byerly, season 1, episode 2, Warner Brothers, 2011.

52. Television Series

Simmons, Nathaniel, director. *Bitch Slap Education*. Fake

Studios, 2010.

53. Specific Performance or Part of a TV Show

"Tired AF." *Bitch Slap Education*, created by Nathaniel

Simmons and John C. Byerly, performance by Jane Doe,

season 5, episode 1. Fake Studios, 2007.

• Wanna emphasize some particular mother fucker? Do this:

Doe, Joe, performer. *Bitch Slap Education*. Fake Productions and

Universal Fake Studios, 2007.

54. Broadcast TV or Radio Program

"The Fucking Right Way." *Shit You Need.* Fox, WRIA,

Columbus, 20 Mar. 2010.

55. Music Videos

Byerly, John C. "Fuck You." *Deal.* Virgin, 1990, MTV.

56. Sound Recordings

Simmons, Nathaniel. "Fuck You." Recorded 18 Sept. 2018.

Fucking Tired. Blue Whale, 2019.

57. Films, Videos, or Movies
This shit should be listed by the title, unless you're wanting to
add some fucking emphasis on a performer for director.

Fucking format:
Title. Directed by Name, performances by (if relevant),

Production Company, Year.

The Big Fucking Deal. Directed by John C. Byerly,

performances by Nathaniel Simmons and Jane Doe, Warner

Brothers, 2000.

Simmons, Nathaniel, director. *The Second Bitch Slap.* Twentieth

Century Fucks, 2015.

58. Performances (operas, ballet, shit like that)

Romeo and Juliet. By William Shakespeare, Directed by John C.

Byerly. Performed by Nathaniel Simmons and John C.

Byerly. Columbus Theater, 22 Feb. 2011.

59. Podcast

"Best of Bitch Slapping." *Bitch Slap MLA!* from XYZ, 3 June

2000, www.xyz.org/podcasts/2343/notrealbitch.

60. Song or Album
This shit will be cited differently dependent upon where the hell you found it. It all depends on that container shit.

Fucking format:
Author. "Title." *Album Title*. Publisher, Publication Date.

CD Example:
John C. Byerly. "Bitch Slap MLA." *Slap*, Columbus Records,

2017.

Spotify (or similar shit) Example:
John C. Byerly. "Bitch Slap MLA." *Slap*, Columbus Records,

2017. *Spotify*, open.spotify.com/track/23432/fake.

Online Album Example:
John C. Byerly. "Bitch Slap MLA." *Slap*, Columbus Records,

2017, www.byerly.com/album/slap/.

61. Painting, Sculpture, or Photograph

Fucking format:
Author. *Title of Work*. Composition Date, Medium of Piece,

    Location Housed, Location of Institution.

Example:
Simmons, Nathaniel. *The Fugly Family*. 1700, oil on canvas,

    Museum of Art, New York.

• Wanna cite an image of an artwork from a fucking book?

Example:
Simmons, Nathaniel. *The Fugly Family*. 1700, oil on canvas,

    Museum of Art, New York. *Fugly Throughout Time*, 9th ed.,

    by John C. Byerly, Fake P, p. 800.

*Is this shit online? Do this:

Online Example (but the shit exists physically):
Simmons, Nathaniel. *Bitch Slap Machine*. 2020. Museum of

    Fake Items, New York. *The Shit*,

    www.theshit.com/archive/bslapmachine.jpg.html. Accessed

    May 2020.

Online Example (for online only shit):
Byerly, John C. "Fucking Boring." *Kill Me Creative*, 1 Jan.

    2000, boring.fakeshit.com/.

7

ANNOTATED LIST OF WORKS CITED SHIT

Truth be told, the official MLA handbook doesn't say a fucking thing about how the hell to make an annotated works cited! Yeah, that's right, the MLA fucking handbook doesn't tell you how to do this shit formally. Common speech is to call this an "annotated bibliography" – perhaps because it is easier to fucking say, but since MLA calls the reference list "works cited" and not "references" or a "bibliography," as we already fucking discussed, we will refer to this as an annotated list of works cited – damn that's a mouthful! Since MLA doesn't formally give a fuck enough to mention how to throw this shit together, it is best to check with your higher power (i.e., professor, boss, pagan deity, or owner) on what the fuck they expect you to do. However, we do have some ideas on how to bitch slap this shit. Just know that we fucking warned you to check with your higher power. In this fucking chapter, we offer suggestions for this shit based off MLA sensibilities (AKA MLA shit).

WTF is an annotation?
Annotations usually include an assessment of the quality of the fucking work related to your specific focus. Annotations may also be a summation of the work and how it pertains to your larger area of focus. For example, let's say you want to compose an annotated reference list regarding "privacy in cultures." In that instance, you should select

research that aligns or speaks to your overarching topic. Within your annotation, after you summarize the shit outta it and such, you may evaluate its utility for your fucking work.

*Annotations are not fucking abstracts, conclusions, or introductions. Nor, should you be a lazy bitch and just cut and paste from your source into your annotation. That's called plagiarism asshole.

Fucking Format:
Annotations generally have a few sentences (sometimes 3-5) that summarize main points within the source. Don't forget to put this shit in ABC order. Based off of MLA's general fucking format, here is what we recommend.

Your annotated references should have two items, in this order:

1. Citation of your shitty source
2. Asshole annotation

We recommend that you double space your shit and indent your annotation so that the works cited info pops like a mother fucking fire cracker. Here's a fucking example:

Gecas, Viktor, and Libby, Roger. Sexual behavior as symbolic

interaction. *The Journal of Sex Research*, vol. 12, no. 1, 1976, pp.

33-49. doi:10.1080/00224497609550920

This article explores how one's sexual behavior is an expression of

one's symbolic environment, as well as how parents and friends

serve as influencing factors. They claimed that language is

instrumental to sexual arousal. The authors argued that sexual

behavior is overlooked in terms of study and, therefore, turned to

Burke and other scholars to explore how symbols are utilized during

sexual behaviors in order to create symbolic interaction.

Notice that your paragraph is aligned with the hanging indent of your fucking citation. This isn't rocket science. Make that shit sparkle!

However, some bitches don't want the constant hanging indent, like so:

Gecas, Viktor, and Libby, Roger. Sexual behavior as symbolic

    interaction. *The Journal of Sex Research*, vol. 12, no. 1, 1976, pp.

    33-49. doi:10.1080/00224497609550920

This article explores how one's sexual behavior is an expression of

one's symbolic environment, as well as how parents and friends serve as

influencing factors. They claimed that language is instrumental to sexual

arousal. The authors argued that sexual behavior is overlooked in terms

of study and, therefore, turned to Burke and other scholars to explore

how symbols are utilized during sexual behaviors in order to create

symbolic interaction.

Essentially, whoever the fuck is making you do this shit needs to fucking clarify exactly what they want, but this chapter gave you two damn good ways to let your shit shine. We prefer the first way because the works cited stand the fuck out and pop like a mother fucking firecracker.

8

10 COMMON FUCK UPS

1. **Using a "magic" website to make your MLA works cited.**
   Don't use a citation generator. They are almost always fucking wrong! Did you not read earlier when we said citation generators are the gateway drug to fucking up?! It's true! Sure, this can be a good starting point, but why not just make it from fucking scratch? Cakes are better from scratch, and so will be your MLA works cited.

2. **Not knowing WTF your Works Cited page is called.**
   That page where you list all of your mother fucking sources is called a "Works Cited" page. Not "References," nor "Bibliography." MLA calls this shit "Works Cited," so use the fucking language of MLA. Works Cited should not be in bold when used as a title of your works cited page. Double space this. Don't quadruple space after your write "Works Cited" or between your references. That shit is annoying AF.

3. **Incorrect Works Cited Order.**
   Put your shit in ABC order. Also, revisit Chapter 4. MLA has a lot of nit picky shit and we sum that shit up there.

4. **In-text citations don't fucking match your Works Cited.**
   This is because something is fucked up. Make sure that your Works Cited are in fucking MLA format and make sure that you are doing in-text citations as you fucking should!

5. **Made up abbreviations.**
   MLA is clear on how to fucking abbreviate different shit. Make sure that you use MLA's abbreviations and not your own fucking concoctions. See the fucking MLA abbreviation list in Chapter 2.

6. **Wrong quotation marks.**
   Know when and when not to use quotation marks in your fucking Works Cited. Double check that shit. Sometimes you use them and sometimes you don't.

7. **Adding a comma between the source and page number within in-text citations.**
   This isn't AP fucking A. This is MLA! MLA does NOT have a comma between the source and page number in the in-text citations. For example, (Smith 33) is correct. Smith is the author and 33 is the page number. Note, there is NO fucking comma.

8. **et al. usage.** Note where the damn period goes. After the "al." Also, remember that this may only be fucking used when you have three or more authors.

9. **Not using the correct edition of MLA.**
   MLA is now in the eighth damn edition. They change this shit up, so make sure you do what's fucking new.

10. **Forgetting to fucking proof your work!**

9

SAMPLE PAPER

It helps to see a fucking sample. Now, we aren't going to give you a paper to steal and call your own. That's fucking plagiarism. However, we do have a bull shit paper that illustrates all this major bull shit we've been talking about (i.e., the first page, levels of heading, in-text citations, and the works cited page).

You'll notice that the sample is short and to the point. This keeps the cost of this book fucking down. The longer the fucking book, the more it costs. You're welcome.

John C. Byerly

Dr. Nathaniel Simmons

BITCH SLAP 101

19 September 2019

Fancy Ass Title

Bull shit. Bull shit.

Pugs

Bull shit. Byerly has argued bull shit (*Forty Years* 50), though he also explained bull shit as bull shit ("American Bull" 34). Bull shit.

Colors of Pugs

Bull shit. Bull shit. Bull shit. Bull shit. Bull shit. Bull shit. Bull shit. Bull shit. Bull shit.

Bull shit. Bull shit.

Fawn Pugs

Bull shit. Bull shit. Bull shit. Bull shit. Bull shit. Bull shit. Bull shit. Bull shit. Bull shit. Bull shit. Bull shit. Bull shit. Bull shit. Bull shit. Bull shit is described as "piles of shit from bulls" (Simmons 5). Bull shit.

Personalities of Fawn Pugs

Bull shit. Bull shit. Bull shit. Bull shit. Bull shit. Bull shit. Bull shit. Bull shit. Bull shit. Bull shit. Bull shit. Bull shit. Bull shit. Bull shit. Bull shit. Bull shit. Bull shit. Bull shit. Bull shit.

Bull shit. Bull shit.

Fawn Pugs are the Shit

Bull shit. Bull shit.

Apricot Pugs

Bull shit. According to Simmons and Byerly, "Bull shit" (10). Bull shit. Bull shit. Bull shit. Bull shit. Bull shit. Bull shit. Bull shit.

Works Cited

Byerly, John C., editor. *Forty Years of Bitch Slapping Advice.* Sage, 2021.

---. "American Bull Shit." Review of *Basic Bitches*, by Nathaniel Simmons. *New Beginnings*, vol. 10, Mar. 2007, pp. 55-57.

Simmons, Nathaniel. "*Speaking like a Queen in RuPaul's Drag Race: Towards a Speech Code of American Drag Queens.*" *Sexuality & Culture,* vol. 18, no. 3, 2014, pp. 630-648. doi:10.1007/s12119-013-9213-2

Simmons, Nathaniel, and John C. Byerly. *Keeping it Real.* Fake Shit, 2016.

BITCH SLAP APA

Bitch Slap APA is Bitch Slap MLA's fucking older sibling. Like Bitch Slap MLA, Bitch Slap APA uses satire and cuss words to teach the American Psychological Association's writing style.
Bitch Slap APA is available on Amazon.
www.facebook.com/bslapapa
Instagram: @BitchSlapAPA

ABOUT THE AUTHORS

Dr. Nathaniel Simmons is a communication professor. As a professional nerd, he researches privacy management (AKA how we keep secrets) in intercultural and health contexts. Dr. Simmons has published his research in (American) national, regional, as well as international journals. He authored *Gaijin Private Parts: Maintaining Privacy at Work in Japan* and co-authored the books *Celebrity Health Narratives and the Public Health* and *Bitch Slap APA*. All books are available on Amazon. Please see his website for his CV and more details:
http://nathanielsimmonsphd.weebly.com/

John C. Byerly is a nurse and graduate student. He co-authored *Bitch Slap APA*, which is available on Amazon.

Nathaniel and John are married and live with their pug, Riblet in USA.

Made in the USA
Coppell, TX
12 February 2020

15742918R10036